Pebble®
Plus

SPORTS STARS

STARS OF BASEBALL

by Mari Schuh

Consulting Editor: Gail Saunders-Smith, PhD

CAPSTONE PRESS
a capstone imprint

Pebble Plus is published by Capstone Press,
1710 Roe Crest Drive, North Mankato, Minnesota 56003
www.capstonepub.com

Library of Congress Cataloging-in-Publication Data
Schuh, Mari C., 1975–
  Stars of baseball / by Mari Schuh.
    pages cm (Pebble plus. sports stars)
  Includes bibliographical references and index.
  Summary: "Simple text and full-color photographs feature eight current outstanding professional baseball players"—Provided by publisher.
  ISBN 978-1-4765-3958-4 (library binding)
  ISBN 978-1-4765-6023-6 (ebook PDF)
1. Baseball players—Biography—Juvenile literature. I. Title.
  GV865.A1S33337 2014
  796.357092'2—dc23 [B]   2013030132

Editorial Credits
Erika L. Shores, editor; Sarah Bennett, designer; Eric Gohl, media researcher; Eric Manske, production specialist

Photo Credits
Cal Sport Media via AP Images: cover; Newscom: Cal Sport Media/Louis Lopez, 15, EPA/Larry W. Smith, 13, Icon SMI/Brad Rempel, 11, Icon SMI/Mark Goldman, 21, Icon SMI/Steven King, 9; Shutterstock: Eric Broder Van Dyke, 5, Matt Trommer, 1, Photo Works, 7, 17, 19

The author dedicates this book to her father, who served as her reliable assistant during the 2001 National Baseball Hall of Fame induction press conferences.

Note to Parents and Teachers

The Sports Stars set supports national social studies standards related to people, places, and culture. This book describes and illustrates stars of professional baseball. The images support early readers in understanding the text. The repetition of words and phrases helps early readers learn new words. This book also introduces early readers to subject-specific vocabulary words, which are defined in the Glossary section. Early readers may need assistance to read some words and to use the Table of Contents, Glossary, Read More, Internet Sites, and Index sections of the book.

Printed in China by Nordica.
1013/CA21301922
092013   007747NORDS14

Table of Contents

Play Ball!

Every spring, fans fill stadiums across the country. They watch their favorite baseball stars smash grand slams and strike out batters.

Pitchers and Catchers

Roy Halladay is a star pitcher.

He is one of only 23 MLB

pitchers to have thrown

a perfect game.

MLB stands for
Major League Baseball.

Justin Verlander is a winning pitcher. He won the Triple Crown of pitching. He led the AL in wins, strikeouts, and earned run average in a season.

AL stands for American League.

8

Catcher Joe Mauer plays

for the Minnesota Twins.

He's the only MLB catcher

to win three batting titles.

Infielders

First baseman Albert Pujols is a power hitter. He hit 30 or more home runs in each of his first 10 seasons.

Second baseman Robinson Canó smashes home runs. He hit 32 to win an All-Star Home Run Derby. The contest is held each year before the All-Star Game.

Third baseman Miguel Cabrera
won a Triple Crown title.
Triple crown winners lead
in batting average, home runs,
and RBIs in a season.

RBI stands for
run batted in.

17

Outfielders

Center fielder Matt Kemp shines on the field and at the plate. He blasted 39 home runs to top the NL one season.

NL stands for National League.

Carlos González is a star hitter and outfielder. He holds an NL batting title. He also won two Gold Gloves as a left fielder.

Glossary

batting average—the number of hits a batter gets, divided by his number of at bats

batting title—an award given to the league's best batter

Gold Glove—an award given to players for outstanding play at field positions

grand slam—a home run hit with runners on all three bases; a grand slam scores four runs

home run—a hit in baseball that allows the batter to touch all the bases and score a run

perfect game—when a pitcher pitches a game where no players from the other team reach base

stadium—a big building where sports teams play

strikeout—three strikes make an out; a strike happens when a pitched ball is swung at and missed, is in the strike zone but not swung at, or is hit foul

Triple Crown—an award for the player who led the league in batting average, home runs, and runs batted in

Triple Crown of pitching—an award for the pitcher who led the league in wins, strikeouts, and earned run average

Read More

Clay, Kathryn. *Cool Baseball Facts*. Cool Sports Facts. Mankato, Minn.: Capstone Press, 2011.

Gagne, Tammy. *Roy Halladay*. A Robbie Reader. Hockessin, Del.: Mitchell Lane Publishers, 2012.

Savage, Jeff. *Justin Verlander*. Amazing Athletes. Minneapolis: Lerner Publications, 2013.

Internet Sites

FactHound offers a safe, fun way to find Internet sites related to this book. All of the sites on FactHound have been researched by our staff.

Here's all you do:

Visit *www.facthound.com*

Type in this code: 9781476539584

 Index

Word Count: 205
Grade: 1
Early-Intervention Level: 19